The Merry Wives of Windsor

by William Shakespeare adapted by Charles Jeffries and Jerry Knight

100 Chauncy Street
Boston MA 02111-1783

Western States Representative
Samuel French, Inc.
7623 Sunset Blvd.
Hollywood CA 90046

Canadian Representative
Samuel French, Ltd.
100 Lombard St., Lower Level
Toronto, M5C 1M3 Canada

NOTICE

THE MERRY WIVES OF WINDSOR

This adaptation of Shakespeare's *The Merry Wives of Windsor* was first produced at MacArthur High School in San Antonio, TX in 1992. Directors were Charles Jeffries and Jerry Knight. The cast included Deborah Banford, Karin Wallace, Paul Merino, Matt Neese, Juan Rodriquez, Will Newcomb, Robyn Reavis, John Norsworthy, Anne-Kathleen Kreger, Anne Vega, Devin Fountain, Steve Anderson, Cody Kennison, and Sean Stanley. The crew included Jason German, Erin Hanna, Kelly Skiles, Karen Hooper, Patti Neff, Alex Sanchez, and Steve Emory.

CHARACTERS

MISTRESS PAGE
MISTRESS FORD
SIR JOHN FALSTAFF
MASTER FORD
MASTER PAGE
PISTOL – Friend to Falstaff
NYM – Friend to Falstaff
MISTRISS QUICKLY – Servant to Dr. Caius, a Frenchman
FENTON – A Young Gentleman
ROBIN – Servant to Falstaff
ANNE PAGE – Daughter to Master and Mistress Page
DR. CAIUS – A suitor to Anne Page
SERVANTS, EXTRAS.

THE MERRY WIVES OF WINDSOR

SCENE 1

(*As the curtain goes up, light music is heard, like a music box. Light slowly comes up stage right and we see a woman reading a letter. She reacts as if insulted by what she reads and speaks:*)

MISTRESS PAGE. What, have I scaped love-letters in the holiday-time of my beauty, and am I now a subject of them? Let me see ... (*Reads.*) 'Ask me no reason why ... '

(*At this point, a light comes up in c, where a rather pudgy older man is seated at a table laboring over a letter with ink and quill. He speaks.*)

FALSTAFF. 'I Love You.'

(*He completes his wording for the letter. A light comes up on stage left, and we see another woman reading a letter.*)

MISTRESS FORD. 'You are not young ... (*She is unhappy at that.*) ...

FALSTAFF. 'Neither am I ... '

MISTRESS FORD. 'Go to, then there's sympathy ... '

MISTRESS PAGE. 'You are merry ... '

FALSTAFF. 'So am I ... '

MISTRESS FORD. 'I say ... '

FALSTAFF. ' ... Love me ... '

MISTRESS PAGE. 'By me, thine own true knight ... '

MISTRESS FORD. 'By day or night, or any ... '

MISTRESS PAGE. ' ... kind of light ... '

FALSTAFF. 'With all his might ... '

MISTRESS PAGE. 'For thee to fight! ... '

BOTH LADIES. "John Falstaff!"

FALSTAFF. (*Finishing up the letter and holding it up.*) They shall be my East and West Indies ... I will trade to them both!" (*He exits.*)

MISTRESS FORD. O wicked ...

MISTRESS PAGE. Wicked ...

BOTH LADIES. World!

MISTRESS FORD. He dares in this manner to assay me? Why, he has not been thrice in my company!

MISTRESS PAGE. What shall I say to him?

BOTH LADIES. Heaven, forgive me!

MISTRESS FORD. (*Plotting.*) How shall I be revenged on him?

MISTRESS PAGE. For revenged I will be ...

BOTH. As sure as his guts are made of puddings. (*Both ladies cross to centerstage, speaking at the same time.*)

MISTRESS FORD. Mistress Page! I was going to your house ...

MISTRESS PAGE. Mistress Ford! Trust me, I was coming to you ... (*They are facing one another.*) You look very ill ...

MISTRESS FORD. Oh, Mistress Page, give me some counsel!

MISTRESS PAGE. What's the matter, woman?

MISTRESS FORD. Oh, woman, if it were not for one trifling respect, I could come to such honor! Perceive how I might be ... knighted. (*Hands letter to her who reads as she speaks.*) I shall think the worse of fat men, as long as I have an eye to make a difference of men's liking. How shall I be revenged on him? I think the best way were to entertain him with hope, till the wicked fires of lust have melted him in his own grease ... did you ever hear the like?

MISTRESS PAGE. Letter for letter, but that the name of Page and Ford differs. (*Holding up her letter.*) Here's the twin brother of your letter. I warrant he hath a thousand of these letters, writ with blank space for different names. (*Fuming.*) Let's be revenged on him. (*Thinking.*) Let's appoint him a meeting; give him a show of comfort

in his suit; and lead him on.

MISTRESS FORD. Oh, that my husband saw this letter. It would give eternal food to his jealousy.

MISTRESS PAGE. Why look here he comes.

MISTRESS FORD. Let's consult together against this greasy knight. Come hither! (*They exit. Enter Master Ford, Pistol, and Nym.*)

MASTER FORD. Well, I hope it is not so, friend Pistol and Nym!

PISTOL. Hope is a cur tail dog in some affairs.

NYM. Sir John affects your wife, Master Ford!

MASTER FORD. Why, sir? My wife is not young.

NYM. He woos both high and low, both rich and poor.

PISTOL. Both young and old, one with another, Ford.

MASTER FORD. Loves my wife?

PISTOL. With liver burning hot.

NYM. Take heed ... (*Holds hand out for money. Ford gives him bag of coins.*) Have eye open, for thieves do foot by night. (*They exit.*)

MASTER FORD. I will be patient; I will find this out. (*Mistresses Ford and Page enter.*)

MISTRESS FORD. Now, now, sweet husband. Why are you melancholy?

MASTER FORD. I melancholy? I am not melancholy. Get you home ... Go!

MISTRESS FORD. Faith, you have some crotchets in your head now. Will you go Mistress Page?

MISTRESS PAGE. You'll come to dinner? (*Enter Mistress Quickly. Mistress Page, aside to Mistress Ford.*) Look who comes. She shall be our messenger to this paltry knight.

MISTRESS FORD. (*Aside to Mistress Page.*) Trust me, I thought on her, she will fill it.

MISTRESS PAGE. You are come to see my daughter, Anne?

MISTRESS QUICKLY. Ay, indeed; and I pray, how does good Mistress Anne?

MISTRESS PAGE. Go in with us and see. We will have an hour's talk with you. (*They all exit.*)

MASTER FORD. I do not misdoubt my wife, but I would

be loath to turn them together. A man may be too confident. I would have nothing lie on my head. I cannot be thus satisfied. (*He exits.*)

SCENE 2

(*Home of Dr. Caius. Mistress Quickly is having a little drink. Fenton enters and calls to her.*)

FENTON. Mistress Quickly? (*Mistress Quickly hides the bottle down her ample bossom.*)

MISTRESS QUICKLY. (*She knows who it is, but ...*) Who's there, I trust? Come here, come here ...

FENTON. How now, good woman. How do you?

MISTRESS QUICKLY. The better that it pleases your worship to ask.

FENTON. What news? How does pretty Mistress Anne?

MISTRESS QUICKLY. In truth, sir ... and she is pretty, and honest, and gentle ... and one that is your friend, I can tell you that by the way. I praise heaven for it.

FENTON. Shall it do any good, do you think ... shall I lose my suit?

MISTRESS QUICKLY. Faith, sir ... all is in his hands above. But not withstanding, Master Fenton, I'll be sworn on a book she love you. Has not your worship a wart above his eye?

FENTON. (*Not wanting to be reminded.*) Yes, indeed I have. What of it?

MISTRESS QUICKLY. Well, thereby hangs a tale. We had an hour's talk of that wart ... ah, but ... go to!

FENTON. Well, I shall see her today. (*Offers her a bag of money.*) There's money for you; let me have your voice in my behalf. If you see her before me, commend me.

MISTRESS QUICKLY. Will I? And I will tell your worship more of the wart the next time we have confidence, and also of other wooers. (*Fenton exits and Mistress Quickly deposits the money into her ample bossom and also exits.*)

SCENE 3

(A room at the Garter Inn. Falstaff enters. He sits at a table and begins to drink from a drink left by someone else. Mistress Quickly enters.)

MISTRESS QUICKLY. Give your worship good morrow.

FALSTAFF. (*Surprised, he chokes on his drink.*) Good morrow ... (*She has no money and is not good looking.*) ... good wife.

MISTRESS QUICKLY. Not so. I be the same as my mother was ... the first hour I was born.

FALSTAFF. I do believe the swearer. What would you?

MISTRESS QUICKLY. There is one Mistress Ford ... (*He becomes excited.*) sir. I pray, come a little nearer this way. (*She is playing with him, since he insulted her earlier.*)

FALSTAFF. I warrent thee, nobody hears. (*He is very impatient.*) Well ... Mistress Ford ... what of her?

MISTRESS QUICKLY. Marry, this is the short ... and the long of it. You have brought her into such a canaries as tis wonderful ... I warrant you, all is (*Gesture of some sort.*) ... one with her.

FALSTAFF. But what says she to me? Be brief my good she –

MISTRESS QUICKLY. Marry, she hath received your letter ... for the which she thanks you a thousand times ... and she give me to notify that her husband will be absent from his house between ten and eleven.

FALSTAFF. Ten and eleven? (*Happy.*) Ten and eleven! Woman commend me to her ... I will not fail her.

MISTRESS QUICKLY. Why, you say well. But I have another mesenger to your worship. Mistress Page hath her hearty commendations to you too ... (*This makes him very happy.*) ... and she bade me tell your worship; that her husband is seldom from home, but, she hopes, there will come a time ... (*She winks at him.*)

FALSTAFF. I pray thee, tell me this ... has Ford's wife and Page's wife acquainted each other how they ... love me?

MISTRESS QUICKLY. That were a jest indeed! They have not so little grace.

FALSTAFF. Fare thee well .. commend me to them both ... separately ... I am yet thy debtor. (*Quickly exits.*) This news distracts me. (*Looks at his face in the drink and says ..*) Good body, I thank thee. (*He dances around as master Ford enters disguised as Master Brook.*)

MASTER FORD. Bless you, sir!

FALSTAFF. And you, sir! (*Worried.*) Would you speak with me?

MASTER FORD. I make bold to press upon you.

FALSTAFF. You are welome. What's your will?

MASTER FORD. Sir, I am a gentleman that have spent much ... (*Falstaff becomes more interesed.*) My name is ... Master Brook.

FALSTAFF. Good Master Brook ... I desire more acquaintance of you.

MASTER FORD. Good Sir John, I sue for yours, for they say, if money go before, all ways do lie open.

FALSTAFF. Money is a good soldier, sir, and ... (*Loudly.*) Will on!

MASTER FORD. I will be brief with you, sir.

FALSTAFF. Very well, sir, proceed.

MASTER FORD. There is a gentlewoman in this town ... her husband's name is Ford ... do you know Ford, sir?

FALSTAFF. I know him not. (*Worried.*) Well ... sir?

MASTER FORD. I have long loved her, and, I protest to you, bestow'd much on her.

FALSTAFF. Have you received no promise of satisfaction at her hands?

MASTER FORD. Never.

FALSTAFF. Of what quality was your love, then?

MASTER FORD. Like a fair house built on another man's ground.

FALSTAFF. To what purpose have you unfolded this to me?

MASTER FORD. You are a gentleman of excellent breeding. There is money. (*Gives him a sack of coins.*) Spend all I have. Lay an amiable siege to the honesty of

this Ford's wife.

FALSTAFF. (*Not clear.*) Would it apply well that I should win what you would enjoy?

MASTER FORD. O, understand my drift. She dwells so securely on the excellency of her honor, that the folly of my soul dares not present itself; now, could I come to her with any detection in my hand ... I could drive her then from the ward of her purity, her reputation. What say you to't, Sir John?

FALSTAFF. Master Brook, I will first make bold with your money ... next give me your hand, and last, as I am a gentleman, you shall ... if you will ... enjoy Ford's wife!

MASTER FORD. (*Not really happy.*) O, good, sir!

FALSTAFF. By her own appointment, even as you came in to me, her assistant, or go-between parted from me. I say, I shall be with her between ten and eleven ... for at that time, the jealous rascally knave, her husband, will be forth. (*Ford is having a difficult time staying in the Brook character.*) Thy shalt lie with his wife! (*He exits.*)

MASTER FORD. My wife hath sent for him? Heaven be praised for my jealousy. I will prevent this. Better three hours too soon than one minute too late. (*He exits.*)

SCENE 3

(*A room in Ford's house. Enter Servants with basket followed by Mistresses Ford and Page. The basket must be prepared so the bottom appears to fall out when the servants try to lift it with Falstaff inside. This way a comic effect is achieved by having Falstaff tip-toe out with the servants appearing to carry him in the basket.*)

MISTRESS PAGE. Come, come, come, come ...

MISTRESS FORD. Here, set it down. Be gone, and come when you are called. And do what we have told you. Mistress Page, remember you your cue.

MISTRESS PAGE. I warrant thee, if I do not act it, hiss me. (*Exits.*)

MISTRESS FORD. Go to, then. We'll teach him to know turtles from jays. (*Enter Falstaff.*)

FALSTAFF. Why now, let me die. This is the period of my ambition. O blesssed hour.

MISTRESS FORD. O sweet John.

FALSTAFF. Mistress Ford, I cannot waste time, I want you for my lady.

MISTRESS FORD. I, your lady, Sir John? I thought you had ambitions for Mistress Page.

FALSTAFF. You might as well think I love to walk, which is hateful to me.

MISTRESS FORD. Well, heaven knows how I love you, and you shall one day find it. (*Servant off.*)

SERVANT. Mistress Ford, Mistress Ford! Here's Mistress Page, at the door, looking wildly, and would speak with you.

FALSTAFF. She cannot see me here. I will ensconce me behind the arras.

MISTRESS FORD. Pray do, Sir John. She's a very tattling woman. (*Falstaff hides behind something on stage, or simply turns away and doubles up. Mistress Page enters.*) Mistress Page, what's the matter?

MISTRESS PAGE. Mistress Ford, what have you done? You are undone forever!

MISTRESS FORD. What's the matter, Mistress Page?

MISTRESS PAGE. Your husband's coming!

MISTRESS FORD. What shall I do? There is a gentleman, good friend, and I fear not for my own shame so much as for his peril.

MISTRESS PAGE. You cannot hide him! Look! Here's a basket. If he has any honor, at all, he may hide in it.

MISTRESS FORD. Oh, he's far too big to fit in there!

FALSTAFF. (*Coming out of hiding.*) Let me see 't. Let me see't. I'll in .. I'll in .. (*He gets in the basket. The ladies cover him with dirty linen.*)

MISTRESS PAGE. Call your servants, Mistress Ford. (*Mistress Ford calls in servants. Enter Servants.*)

MISTRESS FORD. Go, take up these clothes quickly. Carry them to the laudress ... quickly ... go ... (*Enter Master Ford, Page, Cauis.*)

MASTER FORD. Pray you, come near. If I suspect without cause, why then make sport of me; then let me be your jest; I deserve it. How now! Whither bear you this? (*The Servants are still struggling to lift the basket.*)

SERVANT. To the laundress ...

MISTRESS FORD. Why what have you to do whither they bear it?

MASTER FORD. (*Begins to seach for his keys. While he is distracted the Servants lift the basket and Sir John's legs come out and they exit off. He finds his keys and turns to to his friends and says:*) Here be my keys. Ascend my chamber. Search, seek, find out!!!

MASTER PAGE. Good Master Ford, be contented.

MASTER FORD. Master Page, you shall see sport anon, follow me.

DR. CAUIS. This is fantastical humours and jealousies.

MASTER PAGE. Nay follow him, see the issue of his search. (*They all exit with Master Ford, leaving the ladies behind.*)

MISTRESS PAGE. Is there not a double excellency in this?

MISTRESS FORD. I know not which pleases me better; that my husband is decieved or Sir John ...

MISTRESS PAGE. What a fool was he, when your husband asked what was in the basket ...

MISTRESS FORD. Throwing Sir John into the river will do him benefit.

MISTRESS PAGE. Hang him, dishonest rascal!

MISTRESS FORD. I think my husband hath some special suspicion of Falstaff's being here; for I never saw him so obvious in his jealousy till now.

MISTRESS PAGE. We will yet have more tricks with Falstaff.

MISTRESS FORD. Shall we send that foolish, disgusting woman, Mistress Quickly, to him, and excuse his throwing into the water; and give him another hope, to

betray him to another punishment?

MISTRESS PAGE. We will do it; let him be sent for tomorrow, eight o'clock, to have amends. (*Re-enter Ford, Page and Dr. Cauis.*)

MASTER FORD. I cannot find him. Maybe the knave bragged of what he could not achieve.

MISTRESS PAGE. (*Aside to Mistress Ford.*) Heard you this?

MISTRESS FORD. You use me well, Master Ford, do you?

MASTER FORD. Aye, I do so.

MISTRESS FORD. Heaven make you better than your thoughts.

MASTER FORD. Amen!!!

MISTRESS PAGE. You disgrace yourself, Master Ford.

MASTER FORD. Ay, ay; I must bear it.

DR. CAIUS. If there be anybody in the house, and in the chambers, and in the coffers, and in the cupboards, heaven forgive my sins at the day of judgement!

MASTER PAGE. Fie, fie, Master Ford. Are you not ashamed? What spirit, what devil suggests this imagination?

MASTER FORD. Tis my misfortune, Master Page. I suffer for it. Well, I promised you dinner. Come, come, walk in the Park. I will hereafter make known to you why I have done this. Come wife, come Mistress Page. (*They exit, or move across the stage to the outside of the house. When they are "outside", Fenton enters with Anne and Mistress Quickly.*)

MASTER PAGE. What does Master Fenton here? You wrong me, sir, thus still to haunt my house. I told you, sir, my daughter is disposed of. (*Dr. Caius steps forward.*)

FENTON. Nay, Master Page, be not impatient.

MISTRESS PAGE. Good Master Fenton, come not to my child.

MASTER PAGE. She is no match for you.

FENTON. Sir, will you hear me?

MASTER PAGE. No, good Master Fenton. (*Moves away with Dr. Caius.*)

MISTRESS QUICKLY. Speak to Mistress Page.

FENTON. Good Mistress Page, because I love your

daughter in such a righteous fashion as I do, let me have your good will.

ANNE. Good mother, do not marry me to yon fool. (*Indicating Dr. Caius.*)

MISTRESS QUICKLY. That's my master, the doctor.

ANNE. Alas, I'd rather be set quick in the earth, and bowled to death with turnips.

MISTRESS PAGE. Come, don't trouble yourself. Good Master Fenton, I will not be your friend ... nor enemy. My daughter will I question on how she loves you, and as I find her, so am I affected. Till then, farewell, sir. She must needs go in. Her father will be angry.

FENTON. Farewell, gentle mistress. Farewell, Nan. (*Exit Mistress Page and Anne, Dr. Caius and Master Page.*)

SCENE 5

(*A room at the Garter Inn.*)

FALSTAFF. (*Screaming off.*) Fetch me a quart of sack. (*Enter Servant with sack.*)

SERVANT. Here's Mistress Quickly, sir, to speak with you.

FALSTAFF. Come in ... come in woman ...

MISTRESS QUICKLY. Good morrow. Marry sir, I come to your worship from Mistress Ford.

FALSTAFF. Mistress Ford! I have had enough Ford! I was thrown into the Ford! I have my belly full of Ford!

MISTRESS QUICKLY. That was not her fault. She grieves, sir, for it, that it would yearn your heart to see it. Her husband goes this morning a-birding, she desires you once more to come to her between eight and nine. I must carry her word quickly. (*Dirty laugh.*) She'll make you amends, I warrant you.

FALSTAFF. Well ... (*New idea*) ... I will visit her. Tell her so.

MISTRESS QUICKLY. I will tell her ... (*She hesitates,*

hoping for some money.)

FALSTAFF. Well ... get out ... do so ... (*Quickly exits.*) I marvel I hear not of Master Brook. He sent me word to stay within. I like his money well. (*Enter Master Ford as Master Brook.*)

FORD. Bless you, sir. How sped you with Mistress Ford?

FALSTAFF. Very ill-favorouredly, Master Brook.

MASTER FORD. Did Master Ford find you there?

FALSTAFF. You shall hear. As good luck would have it, comes in one Mistress Page ... gives intelligence of Ford's approach ... and in her invention and Ford's wife's distraction, they conveyed me into a ... uch! ... basket!

MASTER FORD. (*Understands his mistake.*) A basket?

FALSTAFF. By the Lord, a basket. Rammed me in with foul shirts and smocks, socks, foul stockings, greasy napkins. That, Master Brook, there the rankest compound of villanous smell that ever offended nostril. Then, servants took me one their shoulders, carried me off, and dumped me into the river!

MASTER FORD. I am, most sincerely sir, sorry that for my sake you have suffered all this. My suit then is desperate. You'll undertake her no more?

FALSTAFF. (*Angry.*) Master Brook, I will be thrown into a volcano ere I leave her thus. Her husband is this morning gone a-birding. I have received from her another embassy of meeting. Between eight and nine is the hour, Master Brook.

MASTER BROOK. 'Tis past eight already, sir.

FALSTAFF. Is it? (*Trying to get Ford out.*) Come to me at your convenient leisure, and you shall know how I speed. The conclusion shall be crowned with your enjoying her. Adieu. (*Exits.*)

MASTER FORD. Hum! Ha! This is what is means to be married. This is to have linen and baskets. Well, I proclaim myself what I am ... he is at my house. He cannot escape me! I will search impossible places. I have horns to make me mad, let the proverb go with me. I'll be horn-mad. (*Exits.*)

SCENE 6

(*Ford's house. Enter Falstaff and Mistress Ford.*)

FALSTAFF. Mistress Ford, your sorrow hath eaten up my suffering I see you are devoted in your love, and I profess requital, not only in the simple office of love, but in all .. but are you sure of your husband now? (*Looking around.*)

MISTRESS FORD. He's a-birding, sweet Sir John.

MISTRESS PAGE. (*From within.*) What, ho, Mistress Ford ... what ho ...

MISTRESS FORD. Step into the chamber, Sir John. (*Enter Mistress Page.*)

MISTRESS PAGE. How now, sweetheart! Who's at home besides yourself?

MISTRESS FORD. Why none, but my own people.

MISTRESS PAGE. Indeed!

MISTRESS FORD. No, certainly. (*Aside to Page.*) Speak louder.

MISTRESS PAGE. (*Picking up on the hint.*) Truly, I am so glad you have nobody here.

MISTRESS FORD. Why?

MISTRESS PAGE. Why, woman, your husband is in his old lines again. He so takes on yonder with my husband, so rails against all married mankind. I am glad the fat knight is not here.

MISTRESS FORD. Why? Does he talk of him?

MISTRESS PAGE. Of none but him ... and swears he was carried out, the last time he searched for him, in a basket ... protests to my husband he is now here and has drawn him and the rest of their company from their sport, to make another experiment of his suspicion ... but I am glad the knight is not here .. now he shall see his own foolery.

MISTRESS FORD. How near is he, Mistress Page?

MISTRESS PAGE. Hard by, at streets end .. he will be here soon.

MISTRESS FORD. I am undone! The knight is here.

MISTRESS PAGE. Why then, you are utterly shamed, and he's but a dead man. What a woman you are. Away with him. Better shame than murder.

MISTRESS FORD. Which way should he go? How should I get rid of him? Shall I put him in the basket again? (*Falstaff appears.*)

FALSTAFF. No ... NO! I'll come no more in the basket. May I not go out before he comes?

MISTRESS PAGE. Alas, three of Master Ford's brothers watch the door with pistols, that none shall go out.

FALSTAFF. What shall I do? I'll creep up into the chimney.

MISTRESS FORD. No, there is no hiding you in this house.

FALSTAFF. I'll go out then.

MISTRESS PAGE. If you go out in your own semblance, you die, Sir John. Unless you go out disguised ...

MISTRESS FORD. How might we disguise him?

MISTRESS PAGE. Alas, I know not. There is no woman's gown big enough for him ... otherwise he might put on a hat, a muffler, and a kerchief, and so hope to escape.

FALSTAFF. Good hearts, devise something ... any extremity rather than an injury ...

MISTRESS FORD. My maid's aunt, the fat woman of Brentford, has a gown upstairs.

MISTRESS PAGE. On my word, it will serve him ... she's as big as he is. And there's her hat and muffler too. Run up, Sir John.

MISTRESS FORD. Go, go ... sweet John. Mistress Page and I will seek some linen for your head. (*Falstaff exits.*)

MISTRESS FORD. I wish my husband would meet him in this shape ... he cannot abide the old woman of Brentford. He swears she's a witch ... forbade her to enter his house, and has threatened to beat her ... is my husband coming?

MISTRESS PAGE. Yes, truly, and talks of the basket too, howsoever he has intellilgence of that.

MISTRESS FORD. Well, I'll appoint my servants to carry the basket again, to meet him at the door with it, as they did last time.

MISTRESS PAGE. He'll be here presently ... let's go dress the fat knight like the witch of Brentford.

MISTRESS FORD. First, I'll direct my servants what to do with the basket. (*She exits.*)

MISTRESS PAGE. Hang him! We cannot misuse him enough. We'll leave a proof, by that which we do, wives may be merry and yet honest too. (*She exits off to Falstaff. Re-enter Mistress Ford with Servants.*)

MISTRESS FORD. Go, take the basket again on your shoulders. If your master bid you set it down, obey him. (*Servants pick up basket and start off. Enter Master Ford, Page, Dr. Caius.*)

MASTER FORD. Set down the basket! There's a conspiracy against me, and now the devil shall be shamed. Wife, come forth ... behold what honest clothes you send forth.

MASTER PAGE. Why, this surpasses all, Master Ford. You are not to go loose any longer. You must be pinioned.

DR. CAIUS. This is lunatic! This is a mad dog! Mistress Ford, the honest woman, the modest wife, the virtuous creature ... I suspect without cause, mistress, do I?

MISTRESS FORD. Heaven be my witness you do, if you suspect me in any dishonesty.

MASTER FORD. Well said, brazen-face. I hold it out. Come forth sirrah! (*He is pulling clothes out of the basket.*)

MISTRESS FORD. Are you not ashamed? Let the clothes alone.

MASTER FORD. (*Digging in the basket.*) I shall find you anon.

DR. CAIUS. Tis unreasonable. Will you take up your wife's clothes? Come away!

MASTER FORD. Empty the basket, I say!

MISTRESS FORD. Why, husband, why?

MASTER FORD. Master Page, as I am a man, there was one conveyed out of my house yesterday in this basket. Why isn't he here again?

MISTRESS FORD. If you find a man there, he shall die a flea's death.

MASTER PAGE. (*After searching the basket, his head comes up and he says.*) Here's no man.

DR. CAIUS. Faith, Master Ford, you must pray, and follow the imagination of your own heart. This is jealousies.

MASTER FORD. Well, he's not here I seek for.

MASTER PAGE. No, nor nowhere else but in your brain.

MASTER FORD. Help to search my house this one time if I find not what I seek, I will offer no excuses for my extremity ... once more, seek with me.

MISTRESS FORD. What, ho, Mistress Page. Come you and the old woman down ... my husband will come into the chamber.

MASTER FORD. Old woman?! What old woman?!

MISTRESS FORD. Why, it is my maid's aunt ... of Brentford.

MASTER FORD. A witch! Have I not forbid her in my house?! (*Calling out.*) Come down, you witch, you hag ... come down I say!

MISTRESS FORD. No, sweet husband. Good gentlemen, let him not strike this poor old woman. (*Enter Falstaff dressed as the old woman, and Mistress Page.*)

MISTRESS PAGE. Come, Mother Prat, give me your hand.

MASTER FORD. I'll "prat" her. (*Beating her on the bottom.*) Out of my door, you witch, you hag, you baggage ...

MISTRESS PAGE. Are you not ashamed? I think you have killed the poor woman. (*He beats and chases Falstaff out of the house. Exit Masters Ford and Page, and Dr. Caius.*)

MISTRESS PAGE. Trust me, he beat him most pitifully.

MISTRESS FORD. That he did. What do you think? Can we, with the witness of a good conscience, pursue him with any further vengence?

MISTRESS PAGE. The spirit of wantoness is surely scared out of him. He will never, I think, tempt us again.

MISTRESS FORD. Shall we tell our husbands how we have served him? I'll warrant they'll have him publicly shamed and I think there would be no conclusion to the

jest if he weren't publicly shamed. (*They exit.*)

SCENE 7

(*Enter Master Ford, Master Page, Mistress Ford and Mistress Page. At the same time, Pistol and Fenton enter from opposite side. This scene is played simultaneously with the action and dialogue switching back and forth between the two groups who are in separate playing areas.*)

MASTER FORD. (*At stage left with his group of Master Page, Mistress Ford, and Page.*) Pardon me, wife. Now does your honor stand.

FENTON. (*At stage right with Pistol.*) Pistol, hear me speak.

MASTER PAGE. But let a plan go forward.

PISTOL AND MISTRESS PAGE. (*At the same time, together.*) I hear you, and will keep your councel.

FENTON. Tonight at Herne's Oak, between twelve and one ... Fair Anne ...

MISTRESS PAGE. ... My daughter ...

FENTON. ... my sweet ...

MISTRESS PAGE. ... and others shall dress like fairies ...

MISTRESS FORD. There is an old tale that Herne the Hunter walks about the oak with great ragged horns ...

MISTRESS PAGE. As this Falstaff shall meet us ... dressed as this hunter.

FENTON. Anne's mother has appointed that I shall shuffle her away while disguised in white ...

MISTRESS PAGE. Let the "fairies" encircle him and pinch the unclean knight.

PISTOL. Means she to deceive her mother?

FENTON. She shall go along with me.

MISTRESS PAGE. The truth being known ...

FENTON. ... and give our hearts united ceremony.

MISTRESS FORD. We shall dishorn the spirit and mock

him home to Windsor.

MASTER FORD. I'll go to him again in the guise of Master Brook and be sure he comes, disguised as the hunter. (*All laugh.*)

PISTOL. I'll to the Vicar.

MASTER FORD. It is admirable pleasure and very honest knaveries.

MISTRESS PAGE AND FENTON. (*Together.*) Let us about it. (*All exit.*)

SCENE 8

(*In the woods at Herne's Oak. Enter Mistress Page, Mistress Ford, and Dr. Caius.*)

MISTRESS PAGE. Master Doctor, my daughter is in green. When you see her, take her by the hand, and away with her.

DR. CAIUS. I know what I have to do. Adieu.

MISTRESS PAGE. Fare you well, sir. (*Exit Dr. Caius.*) My husband will not rejoice so much at the abuse of Falstaff as he will chafe at the doctor's not marrying my daughter. But it isn't any matter. Better a little chiding than a great deal of heartbreak.

MISTRESS FORD. The hour draws on.

BOTH. To the oak! (*The exit to the oak. Enter Falstaff disguised as Herne, with horns on head.*)

MISTRESS FORD. Sir John! Are you there, my deer? Mistress Page, is come with me, sweetheart.

FALSTAFF. Speak I like Herne the Hunter? As I a true spirit, welcome! (*Noises.*)

MISTRESS PAGE. Alas, what noise?

MISTRESS FORD. Heaven forgive our sins!

FALSTAFF. What should this be?

ALL. Away! Away! (*Enter Pistol, dressed in green, with Mistress Quickly, Anne, dressed in white, and others dressed as fairies.*)

FALSTAFF. (*Trying to hide.*) Fairies! Fairies!

ANNE. Away, away, disperse. Till it be one o'clock, our dance of custom round the oak of Herne the Hunter, let us not forget.

MISTRESS QUICKLY. Pray you, lock hand in hand. I smell a man of middle-earth.

FALSTAFF. Heaven defend me ... (*The fairies pinch Falstaff and sing and dance around him. Dr. Caius comes and steals Pistol away who is dressed in green. Fenton steals away Anne, who is dressed in white.*)

MISTRESS PAGE. All the fairies, away, away ... (*They remove masks.*) We need hold up this jest no longer. Now, good Sir John, how like you Windsor wives?

MASTER FORD. Now, sir, who's a cuckold? Falstaff's a knave, a cuckoldly knave. And, he hath enjoyed nothing of Ford's, but his basket and twenty pounds of money.

MISTRESS FORD. Sir John, we have had ill luck. We could never meet. I will never take you for my love again. But, I will always count you my deer. (*Playing with his horns.*)

FALSTAFF. I do begin to perceive that I am made an ass. And these are not fairies? I was three or four times in the thought they were not fairies.

MISTRESS PAGE. Why, Sir John, do you think that ever the devil could have made you our delight?

FALSTAFF. Use me as you will.

MASTER PAGE. Yet be cheerful, knight. You shall eat a dinner tonight at my house with friends, wife, daughter ...

MISTRESS PAGE. (*Aside.*) If Anne Page be my daughter, she is, by this time married ... (*Enter Dr. Caius.*)

DR. CAIUS. Where is Mistress Page?! I have married "une garcon" ... a boy! (*Enter Fenton and Anne.*)

ANNE. Pardon, good father. Good mother, pardon!

MISTRESS PAGE. (*Feigning amazement.*) Why went you not with the doctor, maid?

FENTON. The truth is, she and I, long since contracted, and now so sure that nothing can disolve us.

MASTER PAGE. Well, what remedy? Heaven give you

joy! What cannot be eschew'd must be embraced. Heaven give you many, many merry days! Good husbands, let us every one go home and laugh this sport over by a country fire and dinner.

MASTER FORD. Let it be so ... Sir John ... to Master Brook you yet shall hold your word. For he tonight shall lie with Mistress Ford. (*All exit laughing and talking.*)

* * *